MAKE IT YOURSELF!

PAPER POP-UP *Art*

Pam Chenevert

Checkerboard Library

An Imprint of Abdo Publishing
abdopublishing.com

abdopublishing.com

Published by Abdo Publishing, a division of ABDO, PO Box 398166, Minneapolis, Minnesota 55439. Copyright © 2018 by Abdo Consulting Group, Inc. International copyrights reserved in all countries. No part of this book may be reproduced in any form without written permission from the publisher. Checkerboard Library™ is a trademark and logo of Abdo Publishing.

Printed in the United States of America, North Mankato, Minnesota
062017
092017

 THIS BOOK CONTAINS RECYCLED MATERIALS

Design: Sarah DeYoung, Mighty Media, Inc.
Production: Mighty Media, Inc.
Editor: Liz Salzmann
Cover Photographs: Mighty Media, Inc.
Interior Photographs: iStockphoto; Mighty Media, Inc.; Shutterstock

The following manufacturers/names appearing in this book are trademarks: Bienfang®, Elmer's®, Scor-Pal®, Scotch®, Sharpie®

Publisher's Cataloging-in-Publication Data
Names: Chenevert, Pam, author.
Title: Make it yourself! paper pop-up art / by Pam Chenevert.
Other titles: Paper pop-up art
Description: Minneapolis, MN : Abdo Publishing, 2018. | Series: Cool makerspace | Includes bibliographical references and index.
Identifiers: LCCN 2016962824 | ISBN 9781532110719 (lib. bdg.) | ISBN 9781680788563 (ebook)
Subjects: LCSH: Makerspaces--Juvenile literature. | Handicraft--Juvenile literature.
Classification: DDC 680--dc23
LC record available at http://lccn.loc.gov/2016962824

TO ADULT HELPERS

This is your chance to assist a new maker! As children learn to use makerspaces, they develop new skills, gain confidence, and make cool things. These activities are designed to help children create projects in makerspaces. Children may need more assistance for some activities than others. Be there to offer guidance when they need it. Encourage them to do as much as they can on their own. Be a cheerleader for their creativity.

Before getting started, remember to lay down ground rules for using tools and supplies and for cleaning up. There should always be adult supervision when using a sharp tool.

SAFETY SYMBOL

Some projects in this book require the use of sharp tools. That means you'll need some adult help for these projects. Determine whether you'll need help on a project by looking for this safety symbol.

SHARP!
This project requires the use of a sharp tool.

CONTENTS

What's a MAKERSPACE?

Picture a place buzzing with creative activity. All around you, people are cutting, coloring, and gluing amazing paper art creations. Every supply you can dream of is within reach.

This is a makerspace. It is an area where people come together to create all kinds of cool stuff. Makers share sparks of creativity. They love to learn something new. They work together to design and create amazing **3-D** paper projects. Are you ready to become a maker?

FUN WITH PAPER POP-UP ART

What's the most important part of a makerspace? Supplies, of course! Imagination is also important. Let the materials in your makerspace provide inspiration for your paper pop-up projects. Find ways to make your projects your own.

Some projects will call for certain materials. Don't worry if your makerspace doesn't have all of these materials. Use your imagination to find the perfect substitution for any missing supplies.

PAPER POP-UP ART TIPS

Sharing is an important aspect of a makerspace. Makers share workspaces, materials, and ideas. Being surrounded by other makers is great for creativity. But it also means a lot of projects may be happening at once. Here are some tips for successful makerspace projects.

HAVE A PLAN

Read through a project before beginning. Research any terms you may not know. Make sure you have everything you need for the project.

ASK FOR PERMISSION

Get **permission** from an adult to use the space, tools, and supplies.

BE RESPECTFUL

Before taking a tool or material, make sure another maker isn't using it.

KEEP YOUR SPACE CLEAN

Paper scraps can quickly clutter up a makerspace. Clean up as you go, and store supplies in boxes and bins when you aren't using them.

EXPECT MISTAKES & BE CREATIVE!

Being a maker isn't about creating something perfect. Have fun as you work!

SUPPLIES

Here are some of the materials and tools you'll need to do the projects in this book.

bone folder

card stock

clear tape

computer

craft knife

cutting mat

decorations

double-sided tape

duct tape

eraser

fine point markers

glue stick

hole punch

pencil

PAPER POP-UP ART TECHNIQUES

plain paper

printer

ruler

scissors

scoring board

tracing paper

vacation photos

wooden dowels

Making sharp, precise creases is important when making pop-up art. After making a fold, run a bone folder or other hard, smooth object over the fold.

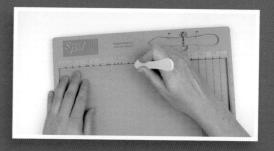

A **scoring** board has vertical grooves at different measurements. Line the paper up with the left edge. Then run the scoring tool along the groove that is at the measurement you need.

9

POP-UP BIRTHDAY CARD

Craft a special birthday surprise
with this cool card!

WHAT YOU NEED

2 sheets of card stock

birthday-themed
foam decorations

pencil

ruler

scissors

birthday-themed
stickers

glue stick

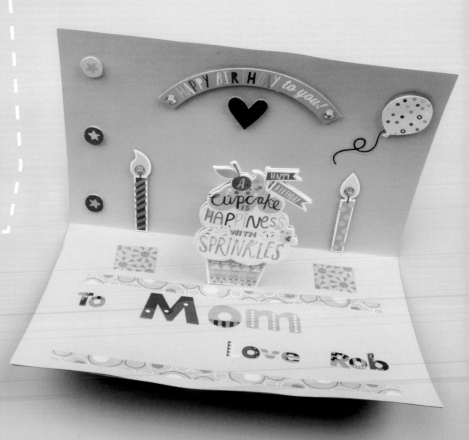

1. Fold both sheets of card stock in half crosswise. Crease them well. Set one aside. Set the other on the table with the fold at the top.

2. Choose a large foam decoration to pop up. Place the decoration on the card near the bottom edge. Draw a line at the top of the decoration.

3. Make two parallel cuts from the folded edge to the pencil line. Space the cuts about ½ inch (1.25 cm) apart.

4. Fold the cutout at the line. Crease well. Turn the card over. Fold the cutout the other way. Crease well. Open the card. Push the cutout to the inside. Pinch the fold to make a square.

5. Glue the pop-up decoration to the front of the cutout. Add other decorations to the inside of the card.

6. Put glue on the back of the card. Line the two sheets of card stock up at the creases. Press them together.

FREE-FORM POP-UP ART

Create a stunning piece of art
with just two sheets of paper!

WHAT YOU NEED

2 sheets of card stock

scissors

glue stick

1. Fold both sheets of card stock in half crosswise. Crease them well. Set one sheet aside. Make pairs of cuts in the other folded sheet to create strips. Cut from the fold toward the opposite side.

2. Fold each strip over. Crease well. Turn the card over. Fold the strips the other way. Crease well.

3. Open the card stock and gently pull the strips up. Pinch the folds so the strips pop up.

4. Put glue on the back of the cut up card stock. Only apply glue to the areas that don't pop up.

5. Line the two sheets of card stock up at the creases. Press them together.

TIP Use two colors of card stock to add depth and contrast to your art!

CITY 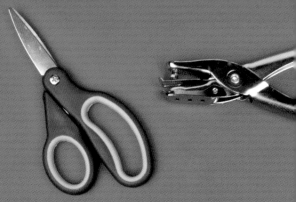 SILHOUETTE

Make a nighttime skyline of your dream city!

WHAT YOU NEED

- plain paper
- ruler
- pencil
- clear tape
- cutting mat
- fine point red marker
- eraser
- 2 sheets of card stock (1 dark-colored & 1 light-colored)
- craft knife
- hole punch
- double-sided tape

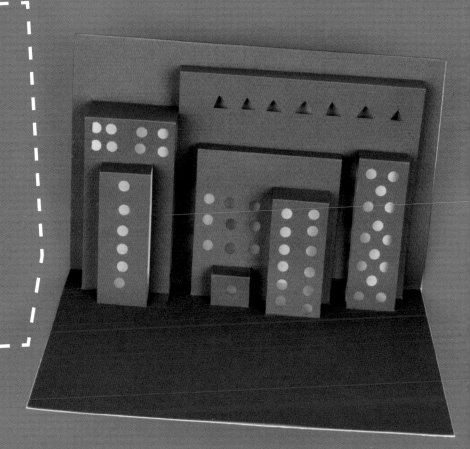

1. Fold a sheet of plain paper in half crosswise. Unfold the paper. Draw a dotted line on the crease in pencil. Tape the paper to the cutting mat.

2. Draw a tall building in pencil. The bottom of the building should be slightly below the dotted line. Measure the distance between the dotted line and the bottom of the building. Draw a line across the building that exact distance from the top. Draw more tall buildings the same way.

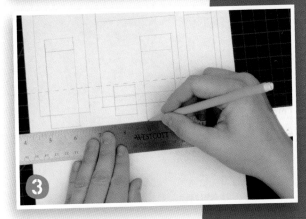

3. Draw a shorter building on top of a tall building. The bottom of the short building should be slightly below the bottom of the building it is on top of. Measure the distance between the bottoms of the buildings. Draw a line across the short building that distance from the top. Draw more short buildings the same way.

4. Trace over the vertical lines with a red marker. These are the cut lines.

Continued on the next page.

Erase any **horizontal** lines that cross buildings near the bottom. Each building should have a line at the bottom, a line at the top, and a line below the top line. These are the fold lines.

6. The sheet with the buildings drawn on it is the template. Place the dark-colored card stock on the cutting mat. Set the template on top. Line up the edges. Tape the template in place at the top and bottom.

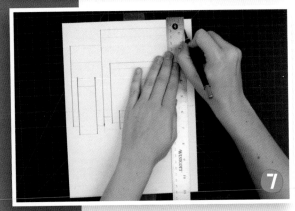

7 Use the ruler and craft knife to carefully cut on the cut lines. Cut through the template and the card stock.

8 Use the ruler and craft knife to make shallow cuts on the fold lines. Do not cut all the way through the card stock.

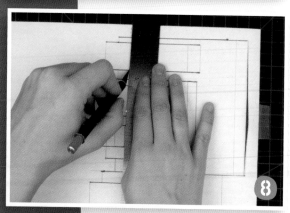

9. Remove the template. Start folding the card stock in half crosswise. Gently pull the cutouts out. Pinch the top of each building so it stands out.

10. Continue folding the card stock in half. Press firmly to crease the fold lines at the bottoms of the buildings.

11. Unfold the card stock. Use a hole punch or craft knife to add windows to the buildings.

12. Fold the light-colored card stock in half crosswise. Crease well.

13. Put double-sided tape on the back of the dark-colored card stock. Only apply tape to the areas that don't pop up.

14. Line the two sheets of card stock up at the center creases. Press them together.

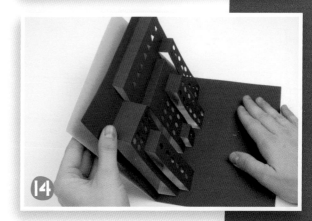

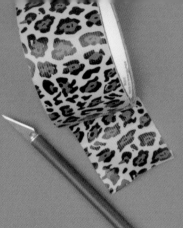

3-D TEAM SPIRIT CARD

Support your favorite sports team with this cool pop-up card that's sure to bring cheers!

1. Type the team name in a word-processing document. Use a bold, plain **font**, such as Helvetica bold. Make the name almost as wide as a sheet of paper. Print it out.

2. Fold a sheet of tracing paper in half crosswise. Unfold the tracing paper. Use a ruler and pencil to draw a dotted line along the crease.

3. Place the tracing paper on top of the team name. Line it up so the bottoms of the letters are at the center line. Use a ruler and pencil to draw a dotted line on the tracing paper across the tops of the letters.

4. Move the tracing paper down so the tops of the letters are at the center line. Draw a dotted line on the tracing paper across the bottoms of the letters.

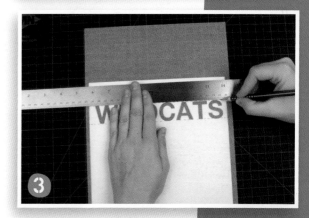

Continued on the next page.

5 Tape the tracing paper in place with the letters between the bottom two lines. Trace around the letters in pencil.

6. Replace the printed paper with a blank sheet of paper. This will help you see the pencil lines.

7 Draw pairs of vertical lines from the tops of the letters to the top dotted line. The lines of each pair should be on each side of an area that touches the center line.

8. Use a blue marker to trace the letters except where they touch the dotted lines. Then trace the vertical lines and the dotted lines between the letters at the top and bottom.

9 Trace the dotted lines inside the letters with a red marker.

10. Fold a sheet of card stock in half crosswise. Unfold it and set it on the cutting mat. Tape the template over the card stock. Line the center of the tracing paper up with the crease in the card stock.

11. Use a craft knife to carefully cut along the blue lines.

12. Use the ruler and craft knife to make shallow cuts along the red lines. Do not cut all the way through the card stock. These are fold lines.

13. Remove the template. Carefully remove the paper cutouts from around the letters.

14. Gently pull out each letter, folding on the fold lines. Then fold the whole sheet in half crosswise and press firmly.

15. Fold another sheet of card stock in half crosswise. Crease well and unfold. Put a strip of duct tape along each side of the crease.

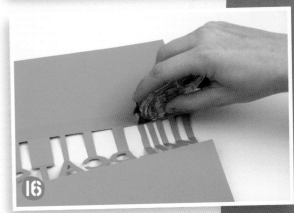

16. Put double-sided tape on the back of the cutout sheet. Only apply tape to the areas that don't pop up.

17. Line the two sheets of card stock up at the creases. Press them together.

SURPRISE POP-UP BOX

Make this fun box to celebrate
any special occasion!

WHAT YOU NEED

card stock (plain &
patterned)

ruler

scissors

scoring board

bone folder

glue stick

decorations

clear tape

mini wooden dowels

1. Cut two rectangles out of card stock. Make them each 10 by 8½ inches (25 by 22 cm).

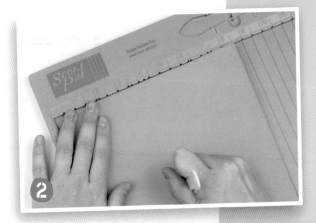

2. Place one rectangle on a **scoring** board with a long side at the top. Score a line at 5½ inches (14 cm). Turn the rectangle so a short side is at the top. Score lines at 4 inches (10 cm) and 8 inches (20 cm). Repeat with the other card stock rectangle.

3. Set the rectangles down with the narrow columns on the right. The smaller **panels** should be at the top.

4. Cut off the narrow column of each rectangle from the top down to the **horizontal** score line. This creates a narrow tab on each rectangle.

5. Put glue on the tab of the rectangle on the left. Press the side of the other rectangle onto the tab. Line the rectangles up at the top and bottom.

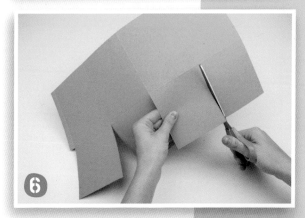

6. Cut along the two remaining score lines from the top to the horizontal score line.

Continued on the next page.

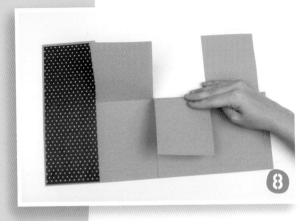

7. Cut a rectangle out of patterned card stock. Make it 3¾ by 9¾ inches (9.5 by 25 cm). Glue it to the left side of the piece.

8. Gently fold and unfold the three uncovered flaps at the **horizontal** crease.

9. Fold each of the vertical **score** lines to the back. Crease each fold with the bone folder. Then unfold all of the **panels**.

10. Cut nine rectangles out of patterned card stock. Make three of them 3¾ by 5¼ inches (9.5 by 13 cm). Make six of them 3¾ by 4¼ inches (9.5 by 11 cm).

11. Glue a large rectangle to each of the bottom panels. Glue three of the small rectangles to the three uncovered flaps. Turn the piece over and glue the other three rectangles to the other side of the flaps.

12. Turn the piece over again. Put glue on the tab. Fold the piece into a box and press the tab to the inside. Be sure the sides line up at the bottom.

13. Cut several strips of patterned card stock. Make them 6 by 2 inches (15 by 5 cm). **Score** each strip 1 inch (2.5 cm) from each end.

14 Fold the ends of a strip on the score lines. Put glue on each end. Stick the ends to the inside of the box. Add the other strips the same way. Space them evenly across the box. Press the box flat to make sure the glue sticks.

15 Open the box up. Tape small decorations to the strips to form pop-ups. Try using mini wooden dowels to make small items stick up.

16. Add decorations to the flaps.

TIP Your surprise box can be a cool greeting card! Just flatten it and put it in a large envelope. Decorate the envelope to match the box.

POP-UP VACATION ART

Make a 3-D scene of your dream vacation!

1. Find or print a photo of a vacation **destination**. It should be it 8½ by 5½ inches (22 by 14 cm).

2. Fold a sheet of card stock in half crosswise. Crease well.

3. Unfold the card stock. Glue the photo to the top half. The bottom of the photo should line up with the crease. The photo is the background. The bottom half of the card stock is the base.

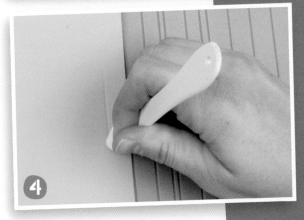

4. Cut a sheet of card stock in half crosswise. Use the **scoring** board to score one long edge at ½ inch (1.25 cm) and 1 inch (2.5 cm). Score the other long edge at ½ inch (1.25 cm).

5. Crease on the score lines. Unfold the flaps to create a platform for your pop-up scene.

Continued on the next page.

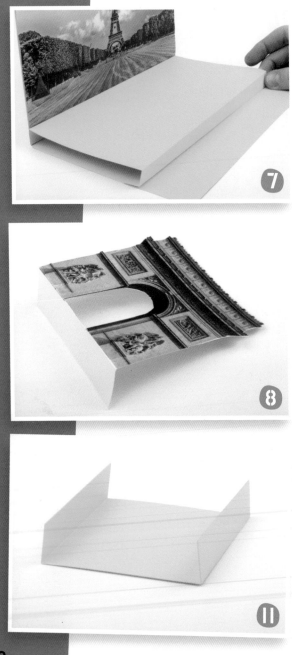

6. Put glue on the outside of the flap on the side that has one **score** line. Press the flap against the bottom of the background above the crease.

7 Put glue on the outside of the flap on the side that has two score lines. Fold the flap under the platform and press it to the base.

8 Cut out several scenery pieces to be the pop-ups. Leave extra paper at the bottom of each piece. Fold the extra to the back to create a tab.

9. Measure how far in front of the background you want one of the pop-ups to be. Add ½ inch (1.25 cm). Cut a strip of card stock as long as the total measurement. The strip should be narrower than the pop-up.

10. Repeat step 9 to cut strips for the remaining pop-ups.

11 Use the scoring board to score both ends of each strip at ¼ inch (0.6 cm). Fold the ends in the same direction on the score lines. These strips are the braces. Keep each brace with its pop-up.

12. Lay a pop-up piece facedown on the table. Put glue on the tab at the bottom of the pop-up.

13. Glue one flap of the pop-up's brace to its back. Hold the pop-up vertically with the other end of the brace against the background. Press the bottom of the pop-up onto the base.

14. Glue the brace to the background.

15. Repeat steps 12 through 14 to add the other pop-up pieces.

16. Glue smaller scenery pieces to the front of the platform.

TIP Hold the background as vertical as possible when adding the pop-ups.

PLAN A MAKER EVENT!

Being a maker is not just about the finished product. It is about communication, **collaboration**, and creativity. Do you have a project you'd like to make with the support of a group? Then make a plan and set it in action!

SECURE A SPACE

Think of places that would work well for a makerspace. This could be a library, school classroom, or space in a community center. Then, talk to adults in charge of the space. Describe your project. Tell them how you would use the space and keep it organized and clean.

INVITE MAKERS

Once you have a space, it is time to spread the word! Work with adults in charge of the space to determine how to do this. You could make an e-invitation, create flyers about your maker event, or have family and friends tell others.

MATERIALS & TOOLS

Materials and tools cost money. How will you supply these things? **Brainstorm** ways to raise money for your makerspace. You could plan a fund-raiser to buy needed items. You could also ask makers to bring their own supplies.

GLOSSARY

brainstorm – to come up with a solution by having all members of a group share ideas.

collaboration – the act of working with another person or group in order to do something or reach a goal.

destination – the place where you are going to.

font – a style and size of type.

horizontal – in the same direction as the ground, or side to side.

panel – a section of a flat surface.

permission – when a person in charge says it's okay to do something.

score – to mark with a line or scratch.

three-dimensional (3-D) – having length, width, and height and taking up space.

WEBSITES

To learn more about Cool Makerspace, visit **abdobooklinks.com**. These links are routinely monitored and updated to provide the most current information available.

INDEX